Made in United States
Orlando, FL
23 August 2022

21475260R00057